come, emmanuel

DEVOTIONS FOR ADVENT & CHRISTMAS 2023–2024

 AUGSBURG FORTRESS

Minneapolis

COME, EMMANUEL

Devotions for Advent & Christmas 2023–2024

Copyright © 2023 Augsburg Fortress, an imprint of 1517 Media. All rights reserved. Except for brief quotations in critical articles or reviews, no part of this book may be reproduced in any manner without prior written permission from the publisher. Visit www.augsburgfortress.org/info/permissions or write to Permissions, Augsburg Fortress, Box 1209, Minneapolis, MN 55440.

Scripture quotations are from the New Revised Standard Version Bible, copyright © 1989 by the Division of Christian Education of the National Council of the Churches of Christ in the USA. Used by permission. All rights reserved.

References to ELW are from *Evangelical Lutheran Worship*, copyright © 2006 Evangelical Lutheran Church in America.

"Household blessings and prayers" are from *Bread for the Day 2023: Daily Bible Readings and Prayers*, copyright © 2022 Augsburg Fortress.

pISBN 978-1-5064-9656-6
eISBN 978-1-5064-9658-0

Writers: Paul E. Hoffman (December 3–7, 18–22), Lisa A. Smith (December 8–12), Jeanette Strandjord (December 13–17), R. Guy Erwin (December 23–27), Stacey Nalean-Carlson (December 28–January 6)

Editor: Laurie J. Hanson

Cover design: Alisha Lofgren

Cover and interior images: All images © Getty Images. Used by permission.

Interior design and typesetting: Eileen Engebretson

The paper used in this publication meets the minimum requirements of American National Standard for Information Sciences—Permanence of Paper for Printed Library Materials, ANSI Z329.48-1984.

Manufactured in the USA.

24 23   1 2 3 4 5

Welcome

O come, O come, Emmanuel,
and ransom captive Israel,
that mourns in lonely exile here
until the Son of God appear.
Rejoice! Rejoice! Emmanuel shall come to you, O Israel.
—"O come, O come, Emmanuel," ELW 257

In *Come, Emmanuel* we join Christians around the world, past and present, in the Advent tradition of reflecting on brief prayers known as the "O Antiphons." Christians have used the O Antiphons since the eighth century or perhaps even longer. Their name comes from the way each one begins ("O Wisdom," "O Adonai/Lord," and so on). The O Antiphons were sung during evening prayer or mass, especially in the last seven days of the Advent season. Around the twelfth century, the O Antiphons became the basis for the hymn we know as "O come, O come, Emmanuel."

 Come, Emmanuel includes daily devotions for the first Sunday of Advent (December 3, 2023) through Epiphany (January 6, 2024). Each of the seven antiphons will be the focus for five days in this book:

- O Wisdom (December 3–7)
- O Adonai/Lord (December 8–12)
- O Root/Branch of Jesse (December 13–17)
- O Key of David (December 18–22)

- O Emmanuel (December 23–27)
- O Morning Star/Dayspring (December 28–January 1)
- O Ruler/King of the nations (January 2–6)

On the first day of each set of devotions, a contemporary version of the antiphon serves as the scripture text, and a stanza from "O come, O come, Emmanuel" serves as the "To ponder" quotation. The next four days in the set include scripture texts traditionally associated with the antiphon and quotes chosen by the writers. Turn to pages 93–94 if you would like to sing a verse of "O come, O come, Emmanuel" that matches up with each day's devotion.

This book also offers an expanded version of household blessings and prayers (see pages 77–89) to enrich your preparations and celebrations.

Emmanuel came that first Christmas. Emmanuel comes to us today. Emmanuel will come again. Rejoice and share the good news!

O Wisdom

O Wisdom, you came forth from the mouth of the Holy One.
Mighty and sweet your ordering of life: Teach us prudence.
—O Antiphon, paraphrased

To ponder

O come, O Wisdom from on high,
embracing all things far and nigh:
in strength and beauty come and stay;
teach us your will and guide our way.
—"O come, O come, Emmanuel," ELW 257

6

Prudence who?

I had to look it up: *prudence*, from the O Antiphon at the beginning of this devotion. Who is Prudence? It is not a word we use much, yet here it is on this first day of Advent for us to consider. Having investigated its meaning, I now understand why it sounds so foreign: one of its synonyms is common sense; another is wisdom.

Imagine a world in which prudence is so pervasive that people and nations live in peace, or a world in which wisdom embraces all things, as we sing in "O come, O come, Emmanuel." Wouldn't that be something?

Advent is a time for such dreams and for dreamers. In Advent we prepare for Christ who came long ago to initiate God's dream of a balanced and beautiful creation—a dream we had ruined with our selfish quest for that which belongs to God alone. God's dream lives on in Christ, and we look for the signs of new creation in the world each day. In Advent God invites us to dream of a world where Christ, who came, who comes, and who will come again, will fill all things far and nigh with prudence. Who? Prudence—the wisdom or common sense that God's dream of a new creation is not a dream at all, but a promise sealed by the birth, death, and resurrection of Christ.

Prayer

O Wisdom, thank you for courage to dream with you of the new creation. Amen.

December 4

Proverbs 8:1, 23-24

Does not wisdom call,
and does not understanding raise her voice? . . .
Ages ago I was set up,
at the first, before the beginnings of the earth.
When there were no depths, I was brought forth,
when there were no springs abounding with water.

To ponder

That which transforms the finite consciousness into the
infinite Consciousness is called wisdom.—Sri Chinmoy,
Life-Tree Leaves

An encounter with the infinite

Wisdom is infinite. When the foundations of the creation were laid, Wisdom was in the presence of God. Even before height and depth were known, prior to water springing from the formless void, Wisdom was around.

Where is wisdom today? It seems hard to come by. We have traded wisdom for quick fixes and easy answers. We have become purveyors of the immediate. We are slow to ponder, quick to act. We forget the lessons of history. Having a world of information in our pockets, we often overlook the power of the slow, the deliberate, the studied. Efficiency has replaced effectiveness. Immediacy is preferred to the gradual.

Advent's gift is a cosmic timeout for those willing to lean into it. I once read of farmers who would take a wheel off their carts after harvest time and hang it above the family table as a frame for an Advent wreath. This was a visual reminder that the family was staying put for a while. After a season of work, the time had come for Wisdom's gifts of rest, contemplation, and an encounter with the infinite.

These are wise gifts to claim if you dare. Challenge the world's holiday frenzy. Experience the ancient, infinite gift of Wisdom's Advent pause.

Prayer

O Wisdom, slow me down that I may know your gift of infinite love. Amen.

December 5

Proverbs 8:30-31

Then I was beside [the LORD] like a master worker;
and I was daily his delight,
rejoicing before him always,
rejoicing in his inhabited world
and delighting in the human race.

To ponder

Wonder is the beginning of wisdom.—attributed to Socrates

The gift of one another

Look at the joy and wonder of the children pictured here
as they put the finishing touches on their world. Just so, the
Creator and Wisdom took delight in each other and in all they
created as the foundations of the world were completed.

We are a source of joy and delight for God. We are lovingly
held and regarded as precious by none other than the Creator
of the universe. But before we get ahead of ourselves, we must
apply the elixir of wisdom: Yes, we are special! Yes, we are chosen! Yes, we are a source of joy and delight for God! And at the
same time, we are no more special, no more chosen, no more
a source of joy and delight than any other person in God's
beloved, human family.

The joyful dance between God and Wisdom, which
Proverbs personifies in today's scripture text, is a great script
for us as people of God to mirror. What if, hand in hand, all
people would find joy and delight in the gift of one another?
Basking in such wonder is, as the great philosopher reminds
us, the beginning of wisdom.

Prayer

O Wisdom, thank you for giving us one another to know and
to love. Amen.

1 Corinthians 1:23-25

We proclaim Christ crucified, a stumbling block to Jews and foolishness to Gentiles, but to those who are the called, both Jews and Greeks, Christ the power of God and the wisdom of God. For God's foolishness is wiser than human wisdom, and God's weakness is stronger than human strength.

To ponder

You pray for the hungry, then you feed them. That's how prayer works.—attributed to Pope Francis

Living wisdom

"We proclaim," Paul begins in today's reading. It is a bold and self-assured confession that with our lives we are giving daily witness to the gospel. Often we are our own stumbling block, as when we say one thing and live in a completely different way.

God's wise and foolish hope about us is that, through the power of the Spirit, we can not only proclaim the words of our faith but live them. Pope Francis's challenge is a good one, especially in this Advent season of preparation hope. There is no wisdom in simply praying that the hungry are fed, that the oppressed are set free, or that the victims of violence find peace—if there is more we can do.

True wisdom leads us to live our lives in such a way as to proclaim the gospel not just audibly but visibly. Where words prayed morph into compassion offered, the seemingly weak and foolish wisdom of God proclaims the crucified Christ. He is risen, visible, and alive most clearly when actions of loving service make our words sing.

Prayer

O Wisdom, lead me to live the words I pray. Amen.

December 7

1 Corinthians 1:28-30

God chose what is low and despised in the world, things that are not, to reduce to nothing things that are, so that no one might boast in the presence of God. He is the source of your life in Christ Jesus, who became for us wisdom from God, and righteousness and sanctification and redemption.

To ponder

Why lies he in such mean estate
where ox and ass are feeding?
—"What child is this," ELW 296

Just to make sure we know

It could have happened differently. God could have chosen to send Christ in a more comfortable way. But "God chose what is low and despised in the world, things that are not, to reduce to nothing things that are."

As one who grew up on a farm, I'm acquainted with places "where ox and ass are feeding." My parents did their best to keep our animals comfortable, but the barn was not a pleasant place. To wrap Jesus' birth story in the trappings of a stall, like swaddling clothes, sends an unmistakable message.

Just to make sure we know, God sends the message from the get-go: the priorities of the Almighty are different from those of the world. The message of the humble manger is further amplified by Jesus' poverty, the despised cross, and a borrowed tomb.

Where do we look for God? We tend to look in places of power, wealth, and beauty. It is well worth it, however, to search with equal diligence in the low and despised places of the world. Clearly, places of poverty, anxiety, unrest, and disease are not places to be glorified. But they just might be the places where God is most clearly and powerfully present, places where we find a new and challenging vision of what God's wisdom can transform.

Prayer

O Wisdom, give us eyes to see you not only in the bold and the beautiful but also in the lowly places. Amen.

December 8

O Adonai

O Adonai and Israel's God, your flame brought Moses to his knees. Your mountain brought forth law and life: Come and redeem us.—O Antiphon, paraphrased

To ponder

O come, O come, O Lord of might,
as to your tribes on Sinai's height
in ancient times you gave the law
in cloud, and majesty, and awe.
—"O come, O come, Emmanuel," ELW 257

My Lord!

Adonai is a name for God that often gets translated into English as "Lord"—a word that gets plenty of play in history and modern culture. Lord Byron, Lord Grantham, and Lord Vader come to mind, and the Lord of the Rings and the House of Lords (upper house of the British Parliament). Lordship is often equated with land, wealth, and power.

Yet for God's people, there's just one Lord, and that Lord is mine. Literally. *Adonai* means "my Lord" in Hebrew. Translated into Greek, the word is *kyrios*, or "Lord," and loses the word "my," which affects the meaning. A lord is one thing; *my* Lord is quite another!

My Lord doesn't mean that the Lord is my personal and private possession, to be used at my will. My Lord, collectively, means that the Lord is with us and for us, always. Adonai chooses to bind the Lord's self to us in love. This makes a difference when we're talking about the law, whether delivered to Moses on a mountain or spoken by Jesus in his teachings. Someone can "lord it over" us with laws. But it's different when those laws come in the context of a loving relationship. The law given to Moses, and to us, is from my Lord and your Lord and everybody's loving Lord. Come, *Adonai*! Come, my Lord!

Prayer

My Lord! We praise you as our Lord of might, majesty, and awe. Help us heed your law and rest in your love. Amen.

December 9

Exodus 3:1-2, 4-5

Moses was keeping the flock of his father-in-law Jethro, the priest of Midian; he led his flock beyond the wilderness, and came to Horeb, the mountain of God. There the angel of the LORD appeared to him in a flame of fire out of a bush; he looked, and the bush was blazing, yet it was not consumed. . . . God called to him out of the bush, "Moses, Moses!" And he said, "Here I am." Then he said, "Come no closer! Remove the sandals from your feet, for the place on which you are standing is holy ground."

To ponder

Staying vulnerable is a risk we have to take if we want to experience connection.—Brené Brown, *The Gifts of Imperfection*

Shoes off

Removing your shoes upon entering a home is a sign of respect in many cultures, but it's also a posture of vulnerability. You reveal your holey socks, or bunions, or need for toenail maintenance. In my house, you'll probably step on a Lego. Shoes off is a risk.

When I taught yoga, some students refused to remove their socks. I didn't push, though socks make it harder to find a solid foundation. There's greater openness—and freedom—in the postures when your feet are bare and connected to the mat.

God commands Moses to remove his sandals. Why? I used to think that particular soil was holy. Now I see that holy ground is everywhere—anywhere where we experience the presence of and invitation from God.

God invited Moses to take a risk, to do a hard thing. How to begin? With vulnerability. With bare feet. With humility. With openness to what God was doing. Without hiding behind footwear or anything else. With feet connected to the holy ground and the one who made it. The same may be true for us.

Prayer

Holy God, you made yourself vulnerable by coming to us as an infant. Teach us to be open to your will, for the sake of Christ. Amen.

Exodus 3:6, 13-14

[God said to Moses,] "I am the God of your father, the God of Abraham, the God of Isaac, and the God of Jacob." . . . Moses said to God, "If I come to the Israelites and say to them, 'The God of your ancestors has sent me to you,' and they ask me, 'What is his name?' what shall I say to them?" God said to Moses, "I AM WHO I AM." He said further, "Thus you shall say to the Israelites, 'I AM has sent me to you.'"

To ponder

"Inuit highly value knowledge of family trees and connecting to our relatives' lives," says Corina Kramer of Kotzebue, Alaska. "In fact, when we traditionally introduce ourselves, we start by saying our name, who are grandparents are, and which village our family is from."—Michaeleen Doucleff, *Hunt, Gather, Parent*

Ancestors

What's your mom's name? This question was posed to me by a girl in a remote village near the Arctic Circle. I was confused by the question; I hesitated. She kept asking. What's your mom's name? I demurred. You wouldn't know her, I thought; she lives two thousand miles away. What's your mom's name? I finally relented. Now that I'm a parent and am teaching my children about their ancestors (in blood and in faith), I see the wisdom and welcome in the girl's question. She was making connections.

When God calls Moses, God reminds Moses that Moses is who he is because of who came before: Abraham and Sarah, Isaac and Rebekah, Jacob and Rachel, and more. Jesus' ancestors are listed in detail at the beginning of Matthew's gospel. Stories of our ancestors can provide inspiration, encouragement, teaching, comfort, and humor. God is I AM, but the stories of our ancestors remind us that *we are*. We experience eternity through the relationships we have with God and with one another.

Prayer

Eternal One, you seek connection. This Advent, draw us closer to you and to the whole human family. We pray this through the name of Jesus, our brother. Amen.

December 11

Exodus 19:18; 20:1-3

Now Mount Sinai was wrapped in smoke, because the LORD had descended upon it in fire; the smoke went up like the smoke of a kiln, while the whole mountain shook violently.... Then God spoke all these words: I am the LORD your God, who brought you out of the land of Egypt, out of the house of slavery; you shall have no other gods before me.

To ponder

The word *love* is most often defined as a noun, yet all the more astute theorists of love acknowledge that we would all love better if we used it as a verb.—bell hooks, *All About Love*

Verbs

It was ten degrees below zero, Fahrenheit, and I couldn't feel my feet. My now-husband and I were Nordic skiing through the woods. I could not stay warm; I was getting panicky. He urged me to stop, eased off my ski boots, and tucked my feet under his coat—and shirt—to warm them. Wow, I thought, this is way better than a love poem!

For God, love is a verb, and that's how the ten commandments start: God tells us what God has done. God brought the people out of Egypt, but that phrase implies many more powerful verbs. God saved. Rescued. Delivered. Sustained. Fed. Led. Loved. You might say one of God's love languages is loving deeds (also called "acts of service" by author Gary Chapman, who coined love-language terms).

We see echoes of this in our lives. Love looks like changing diapers, making sandwiches, clearing away storm debris, cleaning up vomit, piecing quilts, sitting with the person getting chemo, and warming frost-nipped feet. Love also looks like God taking a human form and becoming one of us. Love lived through pain and loss and death. Love did all that first, so that we never go alone.

Prayer

Loving God, your heart is revealed to us in acts of service and loving deeds. Help us to see your great love throughout the scriptures and in our lives. Amen.

December 12

John 18:3-6

Judas brought a detachment of soldiers together with police
from the chief priests and the Pharisees, and they came [to
the garden] with lanterns and torches and weapons. Then
Jesus, knowing all that was to happen to him, came forward
and asked them, "Whom are you looking for?" They answered,
"Jesus of Nazareth." Jesus replied, "I am he." . . . When Jesus
said to them, "I am he," they stepped back and fell to the
ground.

To ponder

May all I say and all I think
be in harmony with thee,
God within me,

God beyond me,
maker of the trees.
—Chinook Prayer

Many names

The soldiers came with weapons to arrest an unarmed man
who was prepared to freely give his life. "I am he," Jesus said, in
response to their request for Jesus of Nazareth. The original
Greek manuscript only says "I am"—a later version added "he"
for clarity. Jesus says, "I am," and suddenly we know: truly this
one is from God, the great I AM.

My third grader asked about the word *Messiah*. I told him
it was another name for Jesus, for whom the people had been
waiting. "God sure has a lot of names," my son mused.

Jesus offers other names with his "I am" statements in John's
gospel, such as "I am the light of the world" (John 8:12) and
"I am the good shepherd" (John 10:11, 14). Those might
resonate with you. Or maybe Savior. Prince of Peace. Christ.
Emmanuel. Healer. Friend. Love. There are many more. The
names we use for God can reveal our greatest longings, our
deepest hopes.

Whatever name we use for God, I AM is coming soon.

Prayer

God, you call us beloved. Whatever name we call you, may it
draw us closer to you and into harmony with others and all
creation. In Jesus' name we pray. Amen.

December 13

O Root of Jesse

O Root of Jesse, tarry not, over all your people your banner
waves. All rulers and nations worship you: Heal the nations.
—O Antiphon, paraphrased

To ponder

O come, O Branch of Jesse, free
your own from Satan's tyranny;
from depths of hell your people save,
and give them vict'ry o'er the grave.
—"O come, O come, Emmanuel," ELW 257

Tender sprout

What do you long and hope for in your own life and in this imperfect world? Join your voice with that of God's people Israel, calling for God's saving grace in your life and over the whole earth. In unsettled times of political intrigue, imminent war, and a breakdown in public life, ancient Israel called for help and clung to the hope of a new beginning. The root or branch of Jesse symbolized God's promised, anointed savior who would bring justice and peace for Israel and all nations. God's promise was Israel's hope. It is ours too.

For Christians, Jesus Christ is the fulfillment of God's promise of a Savior. Jesus, descended from David, a son of Jesse, is the "Branch of Jesse." On earth Jesus faithfully faced the devil's temptations and obediently endured suffering and death on the cross. Jesus, Root of Jesse, conquered the depths of hell and the grave, fulfilling God's promise of a new life. The Branch has become the tree of life for you and all God's creation.

Is your Christmas tree up yet, evergreen with the promise of eternal life? Let it remind you that God is in the growth business. God has a vision of peace and new life, and it will be perfectly fulfilled one day. Tiny baby Jesus, tender sprout, is the root and hope of all the world. Imagine that!

Prayer

Lord of life, fix my heart on your promises of love and new life. Grow my faith and joy in you. Amen.

1 Samuel 16:10-13

Jesse made seven of his sons pass before Samuel, and Samuel said to Jesse, "The LORD has not chosen any of these." Samuel said to Jesse, "Are all your sons here?" And he said, "There remains yet the youngest, but he is keeping the sheep." And Samuel said to Jesse, "Send and bring him; for we will not sit down until he comes here." He sent and brought him in. . . . The LORD said, "Rise and anoint him; for this is the one." Then Samuel took the horn of oil, and anointed him in the presence of his brothers; and the spirit of the LORD came mightily upon David from that day forward.

To ponder

O Holy Spirit, root of life, creator, cleanser of all things.
—"O Holy Spirit, root of life," ELW 399

Rooted

Samuel searched for a new king because King Saul had failed.
Saul did not listen to the Lord but sought his own popularity
with the people. Samuel arrived at the house of Jesse looking
for another big, strapping man like Saul. God had other ideas!
God wanted a king who would have a heart of courage and
faith in God's will and ways. Wet-behind-the-ears David,
lowly sheep herder, was the unlikely choice.

Time revealed that David was not a perfect king. We are
not perfect people. But the key gift in his life and ours is
God's Spirit, the "root of life." This insight from Hildegard of
Bingen is captured in the hymn above. Like David, we have
been anointed with God's empowering Spirit. In baptism God
chooses us, not because of appearance or status, but to give
us a new spirit of heart and faith. Your life is rooted in the
Spirit of Christ, and this gift is renewed in you every single
day. Imagine this: you are imperfect and weak, but forgiven
and made whole. Take heart and trust in God's saving grace for
you.

Prayer

O Holy Spirit, root of life, feed me with God's grace in Jesus
Christ and renew in me faith, courage, and love. Amen.

December 15

Isaiah 11:1-2

A shoot shall come out from the stump of Jesse,
And a branch shall grow out of his roots.
The spirit of the Lord shall rest on him,
the spirit of wisdom and understanding,
the spirit of counsel and might,
the spirit of knowledge and the fear of the Lord.

To ponder

We rally round your newness that is both our hope and
   our work.
Your fearless newness into which we are immersed
 is beyond our expectation.
—Walter Brueggemann, "Do Not Fear"

Fearless newness

The forceful axe of judgment fell on Israel often. There was a "stump of Jesse" because God allowed the Assyrians to defeat and destroy unfaithful Jerusalem and exile the people to Babylon. The prophet Isaiah's words anticipated this cutting down, but still spoke miraculous words of hope and expectation. God is fearless in newness in the face of failure and destruction.

Jesus' death on the cross seemed to be the final cutting down of all of Israel's hopes. But God acted beyond human expectations. Jesus' victory through the cross and over the grave surprised everyone. Dead people did not rise, but God had greater power and imagination than human beings could know. The one who died was raised and his spirit of wisdom, might, knowledge, faith, and life lives on in us and around us.

Perhaps you have had or are having an experience of being "cut down" or "cut off." Failure, illness, loss of a job, or betrayal can do this to us. Remember the Advent good news: God is fearless, fierce, and faithful in the face of all these things and even worse. Join fellow believers in rallying around God's newness. Immerse yourself in it, embrace it, and bring it to others, especially those who are hurting and cut down.

Prayer

God of fearless newness, hold me and immerse me in your promise of healing, hope, and resurrection, that I may be a messenger of hope to the hurting and cut down. Amen.

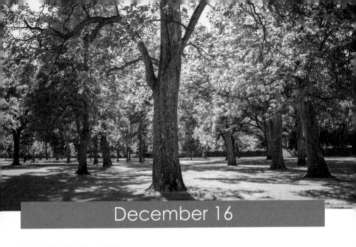

Isaiah 11:3-4, 10

His delight shall be in the fear of the LORD.
He shall not judge by what his eyes see,
or decide by what his ears hear;
but with righteousness he shall judge the poor,
and decide with equity for the meek of the earth; . . .
On that day the root of Jesse shall stand as a signal to the
peoples.

To ponder

To be converted is to know and experience the fact that,
contrary to the laws of physics, we can stand straight, according to the Gospel, only when our center of gravity is outside
ourselves.—Gustavo Gutierrez, *A Theology of Liberation*

Stand straight

What does "fear of the LORD" mean? It is a faithful relationship with the Lord that makes one's life consistent with God's saving purposes. It is a Spirit-led life that concretely echoes God's desires for the well-being and security of all humankind. In Isaiah the ideal king was a public, judicial figure concerned for God's justice and equity among all people, especially those who were poor, meek, and vulnerable. This king was rooted, centered in God's saving purpose for all nations.

Christians see Jesus Christ as the fulfillment of the ideal king. Jesus' "center of gravity" was outside himself. It was in God and doing God's saving will, open to God's purposes and desires.

What is your center of gravity? What enables you to "stand straight" when life presents many conflicting forces and temptations? Do you long for your life to be more consistent with God's saving purposes? Sorting this out, we have one who stands as a signal, Jesus Christ. His life, ministry, death, and resurrection claim and center us. Centered in Christ, the path in this life takes us into the world and the public arena to bring equity and justice for the neighbor.

Prayer

Centered in standing straight in you, O Christ, empower me to speak out and act for people who are poor and vulnerable. Amen.

Matthew 1:1-2, 5-6

An account of the genealogy of Jesus the Messiah, the son of David, the son of Abraham. Abraham was the father of Isaac, and Isaac the father of Jacob, and Jacob the father of Judah and his brothers, . . . and Boaz the father of Obed by Ruth, and Obed the father of Jesse, and Jesse the father of King David.

To ponder

I have learned . . . how powerful a community of trees can be. "A chain is only as strong as its weakest link." Trees could have come up with this old craftperson's saying. And because [trees] know this intuitively, they do not hesitate to help each other out.—Peter Wohlleben, *The Hidden Life of Trees*

Intertwined roots

Trees help one another out, and this makes for healthy growth and a strong community. Unseen, intertwined roots send messages, encourage changes, and share nutrients so that all the trees may thrive. This is the hidden life of trees observed by scientists and forest managers.

What does this have to do with the genealogy of Jesus that Matthew provides? Matthew shows us the very roots of Jesus, the Messiah. We can marvel at the diversity within these roots: wandering Arameans (Abraham, Sarah), lowly shepherds, foreigners (Ruth, Tamar), and a king (David). Here is the mysterious, hidden, surprising work of God.

Advent is a good time to remember God's persistent, faithful work throughout history and in our lives today. God came in Jesus Christ with the good news that all history is in God's hands. God's goal, through Jesus, crucified and raised, is to save the world and all humanity, even in the face of rejection. We are planted and rooted in God's amazing grace. God promises us sustenance, nourishment in body and spirit, and community so all may thrive. Planted in God's undeserved love and in the community of faith, we are strengthened for whatever comes.

Prayer

Planted in your saving love, O God, may I find sustenance for each day and receive the blessings of being intertwined in the community of faith. Amen.

December 18

O Key of David

O Key of David, sign of might, you tear down bars that hold us fast. Deliver the captives and free us from death: Burst our prison. —O Antiphon, paraphrased

To ponder

O come, O Key of David, come,
and open wide our heav'nly home;
make safe the way that leads on high,
and close the path to misery.
—"O come, O come, Emmanuel," ELW 257

Freed from our prisons

Each Sunday in many worshiping communities, we confess that we are "captive to sin, and cannot free ourselves" (Confession and Forgiveness, *ELW*). It's likely those words slide across the page or screen or tumble off our tongues without a great deal of introspection. But pause now to consider what imprisons you. Is it your cellphone? Your preoccupation with self-image? Fear? On which "path to misery" do you most often walk? Surely the responses will be as different as we are from one another, and only as deep and honest as our fears will allow us to probe. But God knows. God *knows*. God knows we are captive to sin and cannot free ourselves, whatever the manifestations of sin that cause us misery.

But the hope of Advent is freedom. Christ's coming to make God visible among us is our Creator's reassurance that our misery is known by God and shared by God. Christ's death and resurrection is the seal of that reassurance that nothing can keep us imprisoned forever, not even death.

So, fly. As a bird set free, live your best life now, free from the miseries and cares that may bind you. Jesus loves you. The way that leads on high is safe. The way that leads through every day on earth is safe as well. Fly!

Prayer

O Key of David, thank you for closing the path to misery. Thank you for setting me free. Amen.

December 19

Isaiah 9:6
For a child has been born for us,
a son given to us;
authority rests upon his shoulders;
and he is named
Wonderful Counselor, Mighty God,
Everlasting Father, Prince of Peace.

To ponder
A good name is rather to be chosen than great riches.
—Proverbs 22:1

Names that resound throughout the ages

There's something about making a name for oneself that may seem untoward at best to us and downright sinful at worst. But if someone assigns a name or title to you, that's different. According to the writer of Proverbs, it's better than money.

Isaiah wasn't the first to talk about wonderful counselors or princes of peace, and he certainly wasn't the last. By the time Jesus came on the scene, people were still talking about those desirable names for a leader. Some thought they fit quite well with this Jesus fellow. "Just look at him," they said—and they said it even *more* after the resurrection. "He's a wonderful counselor, a mighty God. He has loved us like an everlasting father, and the way he calls us to live makes him prince among the peacemakers. He must be the one Isaiah was talking about in the Law and the Prophets."

When we are baptized, we are baptized into Christ. Because of baptism, our last name now, in effect, is "Christian." In the waters of rebirth, we receive this powerful, rather-to-be-chosen-than-riches name.

Advent is a great time to consider how our lives reflect the one in whose name we gather and are baptized. How do we as individuals and as the community of Christ honor and praise Jesus' name?

Prayer

O Key of David, unlock our hearts, our hands, our lips, that our lives may proclaim your name. Amen.

December 20

Isaiah 9:7

His authority shall grow continually,
and there shall be endless peace
for the throne of David and his kingdom.
He will establish and uphold it
with justice and with righteousness
from this time onward and forevermore.
The zeal of the Lord of hosts will do this.

To ponder

If zeal had been appropriate for putting humanity right, why
did God the Word clothe himself in a body, using gentleness
and humility in order to bring the world back?—Isaac of Syria

God's gentle sort of zeal

Zeal often conjures up visions of aggression and power. In John's account of Jesus cleansing the temple, the disciples recall a scripture passage (possibly from Psalm 69), saying "Zeal for your house will consume me" (John 2:17). Upset tables and roving animals end up everywhere.

Writing in the seventh century, Isaac of Syria (also known as Isaac of Nineveh) challenges us to see the zeal of the incarnation differently. God's love for us is so deep, so wide, so all-encompassing, he said, that God essentially laid zeal aside—at least zeal as we know it. Instead of coming in power to establish "endless peace" and to "uphold it with justice and with righteousness," God did something truly shocking. With no armies or weapons, God turned the tables in this way: by "clothing" Christ in a body. It was, in fact, not even an athletic, powerful body like a warrior might have. It was the body of a newborn child.

As it turns out, justice, righteousness, and peace come in the most fragile of packages, that of a tiny baby. It is that sort of humble, vulnerable, understated zeal that unlocks the door and welcomes us home.

Prayer

O Key of David, release us from our lives of power-seeking and open us to your gentle sort of zeal. Amen.

December 21

Isaiah 22:20, 22

On that day I will call my servant Eliakim son of Hilkiah, and will clothe him with your robe and bind your sash on him. . . . I will place on his shoulder the key of the house of David; he shall open, and no one shall shut; he shall shut, and no one shall open.

To ponder

Clothed with Christ in baptism, the newly baptized may receive a baptismal garment.—Holy Baptism, *ELW*

Clothed in Christ

What will you wear to church on Christmas Eve or Christmas Day, or to a Christmas get-together with family and friends? No matter what you wear, the most important garment will be the one that comes from God in baptism. Your baptismal robe is yours for all time, whether the congregation gives a garment or that is implied. This robe cannot be taken away. You have the joy of being clothed in Christ for all eternity.

When Eliakim was appointed the treasurer in the palace of Hezekiah, he received clothing that symbolized his office. Dressed in the uniform of his new vocation, he was expected to grow into the responsibilities and sacred trust that his new wardrobe represented.

We have the privilege of growing into the person Christ calls us to be. Our baptismal clothing is a sacred trust, not a fashion statement. This everlasting garment brings blessing, responsibility, and hope. Christ died and rose to offer all God's creation the gifts of justice, compassion, and peace. Clothed in Christ for Christmas, what doors might we open to bring those gifts to the ones who need them most?

Prayer

O Key of David, how thankful we are to be baptized into Christ. Help us grow into the clothing you provide. Amen.

43

Revelation 3:7

To the angel of the church in Philadelphia write:
These are the words of the holy one, the true one,
who has the key of David,
who opens and no one will shut,
who shuts and no one opens.

To ponder

Good Christian friends, rejoice with heart and soul and voice;
Now ye hear of endless bliss: Jesus Christ was born for this!
He has opened heaven's door, and we are blest forevermore.
Christ was born for this! Christ was born for this!
—"Good Christian friends, rejoice," ELW 288

One way or the other

The church I served as an interim pastor had large, inviting glass doors leading into the sanctuary. Through the glass one could clearly see the font, ambo, and altar and the new life in Christ they promised. Because these doors offered such an inviting entry, and because the sanctuary beckoned, I would routinely stampede ahead, pushing the doors out of my way so I could enter for whatever reason I had to go inside.

There was only one problem. The doors did not push in. They swung out, which anyone could tell from the large, almost foreboding, wooden handles that clearly invited anyone who was entering to PULL, not push. More than once I banged my head against the glass as I tried to push my way in to a door that clearly opened out. It may have even happened on my last Sunday there, after eighteen months of failed attempts to push my way in.

Today's scripture text and hymn verse provide welcome reassurance to people like me: Jesus opens the doors that lead to a life that is blessed and holy. There is no need to push or shove our way in. The one who has the key of David holds the door wide open. Christ was born for this! Christ was born for this!

Prayer

O Key of David, thank you for being open to us 24/7. Amen.

O Emmanuel

O God in our midst, Emmanuel, in you our salvation comes to earth. Come, rule our lives and make us whole: Come and save us. —O Antiphon, paraphrased

To ponder

O come, O come, Emmanuel,
and ransom captive Israel,
that mourns in lonely exile here
until the Son of God appear.
—"O come, O come, Emmanuel," ELW 257

Far away and yet intimately close

For centuries God's people remembered the promise: one would someday come who would manifest God's love and witness to God's power, and bring a new birth of freedom into their lives and world. How, though, could this be? God was impossibly distant, farther than the heavens. How could God be also in our midst, and after all this time?

God is with us when our hearts and minds work together in harmony and are drawn to the good. I have experienced this in teaching and learning—in the compelling moment of mutual understanding we know when a group of us are focused on a task, a question, or a goal. God is with us in our stretching, striving, and learning.

God is with us now as we wait for Emmanuel to come among us again at Christmas.

Prayer

God, open up our minds and our hearts and our senses and enable us to feel your nearness, hear your quiet whisper, and taste the sweetness of your presence in our midst. Open us to newness of life. Amen.

December 24 / Advent 4 / Christmas Eve

Isaiah 7:14

The Lord himself will give you a sign. Look, the young woman is with child and shall bear a son, and shall name him Immanuel.

To ponder

The blessing that the Father planned
the Son holds in his infant hand,
that in his kingdom, bright and fair,
you may with us his glory share.
—"From heaven above," ELW 268

Signs and wonders

Long ago, Martin Luther struggled to find words to describe Jesus' coming to us at Christmas in a way even a child could understand. His famous hymn "From heaven above" was the result, and in its many stanzas he lays out in simple language the marvelous glory and mystery of the incarnation of God in human flesh as Jesus. We still wrestle with this idea today, in a world where the manifestation of God as a helpless child is as contradictory as it has ever been. But the image of the mother and her child still hold their power.

We all long for a sign, a flash of clarity, a sudden insight into a profound truth. But life goes on, each day follows the one before. Someone is born, someone dies every minute—and we persist. And then, on this holy night, it is as though time stands still—the stars stop in their courses and the heavens drop to within the reach of our hands. For this birth is different; this child is unlike any other: this infant is God, with us.

Prayer

O God who loves us even when we struggle to understand you, help us to slow down, and to stop placing things in the way of your love for us. You have broken our world open, torn the curtain in two, and you come to us anew in this holy night. Join us to yourself and fill us with the love you are bestowing on all the world tonight. Amen.

December 25 / Christmas Day

Matthew 1:18-21

Now the birth of Jesus the Messiah took place in this way. When his mother Mary had been engaged to Joseph, but before they lived together, she was found to be with child from the Holy Spirit. Her husband Joseph, being a righteous man and unwilling to expose her to public disgrace, planned to dismiss her quietly. But just when he had resolved to do this, an angel of the Lord appeared to him in a dream and said, "Joseph, son of David, do not be afraid to take Mary as your wife, for the child conceived in her is from the Holy Spirit. She will bear a son, and you are to name him Jesus, for he will save his people from their sins."

To ponder

Rank on rank the host of heaven
spreads its vanguard on the way;
as the Light of light, descending
from the realms of endless day,
comes, the pow'rs of hell to vanquish,
as the darkness clears away.
—"Let all mortal flesh keep silence," ELW 490

Christ our God to earth descending

We wish we knew more about Joseph, whose patience and steadfast support of his bride and her child are an essential frame around the story of Jesus' birth. In the beloved hymn "Let all mortal flesh keep silence," we are urged to lift our minds from earthly things and raise them to the ineffable and eternal glory of God, sung by the angels forever.

Joseph was able, with an angel's help, to do just that. Like Isaiah's prediction of a son to be born to humankind whose name would be Immanuel (God with us), Joseph (and all of us) are taken by this miracle into the realm of the mysterious and wondrous and glorious.

Prayer

God, you are with us today as every day in the person of your Son, Jesus Christ. Fill us with love for you and one another for Jesus' sake; help us see you in one another. Amen.

December 26

Matthew 1:22-25

All this took place to fulfill what had been spoken by the Lord through the prophet:

"Look, the virgin shall conceive and bear a son, and they shall name him Emmanuel," which means, "God is with us." When Joseph awoke from sleep, he did as the angel of the Lord commanded him; he took her as his wife, but had no marital relations with her until she had borne a son; and he named him Jesus.

To ponder

Abide with richest blessings among us, bounteous Lord;
let us in grace and wisdom grow daily through your word.
—"Abide, O dearest Jesus," ELW 539

God is with us

On this second day of Christmas, as we clean up the debris from yesterday and start eating up the leftovers, we may have a few moments of quiet to consider how Christ has come into our world, our hearts, and our homes this season, not just to make a joyful appearance, but to make a home there forever—this day, and every day to come.

This may be easy to feel today, still warm with the joys of the season, but it will be even more important to remember tomorrow and beyond: God is with us in Jesus. In times of challenge and difficulty, God's presence with us in Jesus gives us strength beyond our weakness and clarity beyond our doubts. In the great hymn "Abide, O dearest Jesus," seventeenth-century German pastor and teacher Josua Stegmann reminds us that Jesus is with us in every time of trouble. Himself subjected to humiliation and loss in time of war, Stegmann's hymn is a song of courage and hope in the face of challenges.

Prayer

Faithful God, we live in the promises you make to us, and we feel those promises most strongly in the miracle of the Word made flesh, who we remember and celebrate at Christmas. May this light and warmth not fade; may your presence with us in Jesus always give us courage to live. Amen.

December 27

Matthew 28:18-20

Jesus came and said to [the disciples], "All authority in heaven and on earth has been given to me. Go therefore and make disciples of all nations, baptizing them in the name of the Father and of the Son and of the Holy Spirit, and teaching them to obey everything that I have commanded you. And remember, I am with you always, to the end of the age."

To ponder

The Lord now sends us forth with hands to serve and give,
to make of all the earth a better place to live.
The angels are not sent into our world of pain

to do what we were meant to do in Jesus' name;
that falls to you and me and all who are made free.
Help us, O Lord, we pray, to do your will today.
—"The Lord now sends us forth," ELW 538

Sent forth to make a difference

The story of Christ's coming at Christmas is not just to warm
our hearts with the knowledge and comfort of God's love and
abiding presence, it also empowers and energizes and propels
us forward.

God in Christ is with us always. Now Jesus calls us to live
what we believe. In the Spanish hymn we sing as "The Lord
now sends us forth," that commission to go out into the world
to baptize and teach—in other words, to transform the world
and society around us—is clear. Our call is to love and honor
God by helping others, and to love our neighbors as ourselves
by making a difference in our communities.

Prayer

God of all, you are our loving parent as well as our powerful
guide. Empower us to live fearlessly, to help others without counting the cost, and to bear your love to the world.
Wherever we see injustice, let our voice be clear and our
witness forthright—and may your love prevail. Amen.

O Morning Star

O Morning Star of righteousness, your light shines brightly in the night. Dispel our shadows and bring us light: Illumine our darkness. —O Antiphon, paraphrased

To ponder

O come, O Dayspring, come and cheer;
O Sun of justice, now draw near
Disperse the gloomy clouds of night,
and death's dark shadow put to flight.
—"O come, O come, Emmanuel," ELW 257

Grief's shadow

Christmas lights adorned the college campus the night I learned my brother had died. I walked to my dorm room, knowing Mike was gone even before my mom, on the other end of the phone, spoke the words aloud.

Years later, I wrote: "Lights through tears are a living thing, moving in place, now blurred, now brilliant—magnified. Eyelids close in unbounded regret, squeezed shut in a silent scream. But even then the light lives—rainbows dancing on water, Advent hope magnified."

In the brilliant light of Christmas, death's shadow looms especially large. Grief threatens to overpower hope and trust. In a season that celebrates birth, we are so aware of death.

Into this profound tension, Love is born again and again. God comes to dwell among us, chasing away the distorting shadow that would have us believe that death destroys life. We mourn, but not without hope. The light of Christ—shining forth from the empty tomb—illumines our way through death to life without end. And somehow—by God's grace—light that shines through tears is magnified. A rainbow forms behind our shuttered eyes. God's promise persists, birthing Love stronger than any death.

Prayer

O Dayspring, illumine our lives with your steadfast love and mercy. Where grief overwhelms us, shepherd us through death to life. Amen.

December 29

Isaiah 60:1-2

Arise, shine; for your light has come,
and the glory of the Lord has risen upon you....
the LORD will arise upon you,
and his glory will appear over you.

To ponder

The Christmas gospel is this: despite it all there is joy, there
are celebrations, there are baby showers in shelters and people
who look out for each other and strangers who do what they
can with what they have. This world is held in God's care,
every life held by God. There are always good reasons to sing
a hallelujah, even if we don't know the right words.—Isaac S.
Villegas, "A Shower in the Desert"

Abiding hope

The word of the prophet Isaiah comes to a people who are far from home, exiled from all they've ever known. God's beloved ones are defeated and deflated, plagued by despair, and laid low. Is there any hope? When all is in disrepair, including the human spirit, is there a future filled with possibility?

To the questions of the people—those who wailed aloud and those silently weeping from their broken hearts—the prophet speaks a profound *yes*. Yes, there is hope. Yes, there is a future filled with possibility. Your Lord is here *for you*.

We are not left alone to figure it all out, to make the changes we know will help, to pull ourselves out of the pit and up to steady ground. We are held in the light of a God with whom all things are possible, a God who refuses to abandon us.

This God has come to you already and will continue to illumine your way home. There is no past that is void of God's abiding love. There is no future where we do not shine with the light of the Lord.

Prayer

God, we live in awe of your goodness and your abiding presence beside us through the hills and valleys of life. Heal our hearts this day. Give us the hope that comes through you alone. Amen.

December 30

John 8:12

[Jesus said,] "I am the light of the world. Whoever follows me
will never walk in darkness but will have the light of life."

To ponder

I want to love more than death can harm. And I want to tell
you this often: That despite being so human and so terrified,
here, standing on this unfinished staircase to nowhere and
everywhere, surrounded by the cold and starless night—
we can live. And we will.—Ocean Vuong, "The Weight of
Our Living"

No condemnation

Jesus speaks these words in the wake of a dramatic, world-altering episode. "All the people" have come to Jesus in the temple (John 8:2). As he's teaching them, a group of people shows up intending to test Jesus so that they might find a charge to bring against him.

They do not arrive in front of Jesus alone, but with a woman they've conscripted for their treacherous plan—a woman who, in their understanding, deserves to be stoned to death as punishment for a sinful act. They have no qualms about dragging this woman in front of the crowd and using her as a pawn in their mission to silence Jesus.

Jesus turns their gaze from her; his response to their questioning invites them to look at themselves: "Let anyone among you who is without sin be the first to throw a stone at her" (John 8:7). None of them are without sin. No one can condemn her. No one can condemn you.

"God did not send the Son into the world to condemn the world, but in order that the world might be saved through him" (John 3:17). Jesus upends the judgment we inflict on ourselves and on one another. He surprises us, time and again, with forgiveness and grace, light and life.

Prayer

Light of the world, be at work in us when we are fearful, jealous, or judgmental. Free us for life. Empower us to follow you in the way of love and mercy. Amen.

2 Peter 1:16

We did not follow cleverly devised myths when we made known to you the power and coming of our Lord Jesus Christ, but we had been eyewitnesses of his majesty.

To ponder

There's something to being led. . . . You see, we don't have enough sense to make these decisions. Somehow, you just get led to where you're supposed to be. . . . My father identified this great ignorance for me. . . . We were sitting on his front porch when he was about my age now. We were sitting there, totally in the dark, and he said, "Well, I've had a wonderful life. And I've had nothing to do with it."—Wendell Berry, in "Going Home with Wendell Berry"

God's resolve

There's no end to "cleverly devised myths" this time of year. Advertising campaigns persuade us we're lacking. All will be well if we simply purchase the right product. Life will be good when we follow through on New Year's resolutions.

The power, though, is not in the latest meal plan or exercise fad. The perfect planner won't change your life from the inside out. Consumption, despite our society's fervent attempts to convince us otherwise, is not the path to abundant life.

The true power is in Jesus. The baby born in Bethlehem has been born anew in you through the waters of baptism. The power of God to make all things new abides with you, resides in you, and empowers you to share the good news of God's transforming love.

What will the power of Christ do through you and within you this year? How will the power of Christ empower us all to live and love wholeheartedly?

The power of Christ is not for sale. It's been given to you freely, a gift from your Savior. Thanks be to God!

Prayer

God, you exercise your power through vulnerability, choosing to save us by becoming one of us. You free us to live lives of expansive love. Wash over us again today. Fill us with your power. Amen.

January 1

2 Peter 1:17-19

[Jesus Christ] received honor and glory from God the Father when that voice was conveyed to him by the Majestic Glory, saying "This is my Son, my Beloved, with whom I am well pleased." We ourselves heard this voice come from heaven, while we were with him on the holy mountain. . . . You will do well to be attentive to this as to a lamp shining in a dark place, until the day dawns and the morning star rises in your hearts.

To ponder

Occasionally, we can sense that we're getting swamped by what's beyond us, whether it's the sorrows of the world or our seemingly endless to-do lists. Often, we feel overwhelmed by all that we can't control. . . . Perhaps then, more than ever, we need to be summoned back to what grounds us, to what tells a better story. Perhaps then, more than ever, I need the testimony of the flowers—to receive all over again a reminder of grace.—Jeff Chu, "Arranging the Flowers"

Paying attention

What do you pay attention to?

I was walking on a trail near my home, surrounded by wildflowers gone to seed, the steady flow of a gentle river, and the peeling bark of a river birch tree. "Why not slow down?" I wondered. "What does it cost to pay attention?"

It's a new year, the vast unknown stretching out before us. What will you pay attention to? Will you slow down for truth that emerges slowly and sometimes painfully? Will you seek out the beauty that surrounds you? Will you attend to the voice of God?

God's Beloved has been born for us. The river birch, the black-eyed Susan, the river's current and its rocky shores are fully alive in Christ. Moving into the unknown of this new year, this is what we do know: Christ is our life.

Prayer

Bless this new year with your presence, O God. Through every day to come, be our song, our sanctuary, our delight, and our guiding light. Help us pay attention to the daily miracles that attend our lives. Amen.

O Ruler of the nations

O Ruler of the nations, Desire and longing for wholeness,
come. We are your creatures, you formed us of earth: Save
your people.—O Antiphon, paraphrased

To ponder

O come, O King of nations, come,
O Cornerstone that binds in one:
refresh the hearts that long for you;
restore the broken, make us new.
—"O come, O come, Emmanuel," ELW 257

Hit reset

Have you ever been advised to "turn it off and start it up again" as a way of resetting and resolving whatever technology has gone awry? Isn't it wild how often that strategy works? Wouldn't it be terrific if we had been born with a reset button?

Perhaps we have been. God formed us from the dust of the earth and breathed life into us. All we have and all we are is a gift from our creator. We long to live fully alive. We long to be well. Our desire and longing for wholeness is God at work in us, breathing through us, calling us to abundant life. It is the Holy Spirit who stirs within us through every breath, praying for us that our hearts might be refreshed, that the broken parts of us might be restored, that we might be made new.

The Word of God made flesh in Jesus Christ is this world's reset button, reframing the law, reaching out to marginalized people, bringing our salvation through death on a cross. The birth of the Prince of peace turns this world upside down, resetting all creation on paths of justice and mercy. We trust in the salvation of God, who makes all things new.

Prayer

With every breath, O God, we praise you. With every breath, O God, we pray to you. Tune our hearts to you; put us in sync with your purposes. Where we need a change of heart, turn us tenderly toward you. Amen.

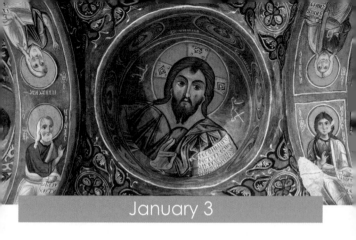

January 3

Jeremiah 10:6-7

There is none like you, O Lord;
you are great, and your name is great in might.
Who would not fear you, O King of the nations?
For that is your due;
among all the wise ones of the nations
and in all their kingdoms
there is no one like you.

To ponder

We are to fear, love, and trust God above all things.—Martin
Luther, *Luther's Small Catechism*

God alone

The people of Israel have been idolatrous. They've fallen for the false promises of false gods. Sound familiar? How often do we think that life would be good if we only had more time, money, influence, and power? How often are we beholden to the fear that we don't have enough of these things?

Jeremiah asks, "Who would not fear you, O King of the nations?" As it turns out, all of us. All of us, at times, look to something or someone other than God for our life and salvation. We do this even though, as Jeremiah points out, "idols are like scarecrows in a cucumber field" (10:5)! They have absolutely no power to save us.

The only one who perfectly fears, loves, and trusts God above all things is Jesus. Trust in God led Jesus through days of trial and temptation in the wilderness, days of incredulity at the fickleness of the human heart, and days of trial and conviction that led him ultimately to the cross. Even there, Jesus trusted God to shepherd him through death to eternal life.

The faith of Jesus is the faith that lives in us, empowering us to trust God and to recognize that our idols are powerless. God alone gives us life.

Prayer

Sometimes we lose our way, precious Lord. We forget that you're faithful. Worry besets us; thoughts of scarcity confuse and exhaust us. Renew our trust in you. Amen.

January 4

Micah 5:2

You, O Bethlehem of Ephrathah,
who are one of the little clans of Judah,
from you shall come forth for me
one who is to rule in Israel,
whose origin is from of old,
from ancient days.

To ponder

You may not think of yourself as an activist, but the river moving for love and justice has many tributaries.—Jacqui Lewis,
Fierce Love

What can I do?

There are days when you may feel small in this world. I feel this especially on those days when I'm overcome by the challenges facing us at this moment in history—climate change, systemic racism, gun violence, and more. I feel as though nothing I can do will make a difference. I fear change will never come.

We may be small, but we are not powerless to make a difference. God is at work in us just as surely as God was at work in that little town of Bethlehem and in Mary, whose song to a world-turning God we sing. We bear Christ in our bodies, pregnant with the possibilities of God. We bear Christ in our voices, sharing the good news with a weary world. Jesus Christ is born! Our salvation is here. Change will come through God at work in us. God's promise is not just a future, but a future with hope.

Prayer

With our lives, O God, we sing your praise. You are the one who turns this world upside down, feeding the ones who are hungry, uplifting the ones who are oppressed, disturbing our notions of what it means to be strong and powerful. Keep on working needed change through us. Amen.

January 5

Micah 5:4-5

And he shall stand and feed his flock in the strength of the
LORD,
in the majesty of the name of the LORD his God.
And they shall live secure, for now he shall be great
to the ends of the earth;
and he shall be the one of peace.

To ponder

Practice peace by trusting, by looking at the map as *one* of
many ways to plan ahead and then taking the path while
holding your plans loosely. Practice peace by slowing down
to notice the other people on the journey who are asking
questions just like you. Practice peace by traveling through the

daily rhythms of life, leaving room for redirection.—Morgan Harper Nichols, *Peace Is a Practice*

Out of my control

I'm not sure I would have chosen the image of sledding down a hill to accompany this reading from Micah. My only real sledding experience was not a secure experience. It probably didn't help that I was sledding on a tray from my college cafeteria, down a frozen-solid hill on our rolling campus. Oops! I felt completely out of control, and that's not a feeling I enjoy.

Perhaps, though, that's the point. Life is ultimately out of our control. We can't know, in advance, where our decisions will lead us. We can't change our loved ones any more than we can change the weather. Given all the potential hazards over which we have no control, how do we sled through life with our friends—with huge smiles on our faces?

If the one in control is trustworthy and has our best interests at heart, then there is freedom in letting go. If the one in control can work resurrection, then we can relax into this unfolding story that is our lives. On every page, the love of God holds us secure.

Prayer

You hold the world in your hands, gracious God. Help us feel your steady embrace this day, this hour, this minute. Give us your peace. Amen.

January 6 / Epiphany of Our Lord

Matthew 2:11-12

[The magi] saw the child with Mary his mother; and they knelt down and paid him homage. Then, opening their treasure chests, they offered him gifts of gold, frankincense, and myrrh. And having been warned in a dream not to return to Herod, they left for their own country by another road.

To ponder

Deep in the night I looked out the window and saw stars glimmering in a clear sky, the clouds all blown away. The trees swung back and forth and my heart pounded, but deep inside me was a quiet place, protected and calm.—Barbara Bash, *True Nature*

The end and the beginning

Bethlehem is not the end of the road for the magi. The star stops, but now God uses their dreams to direct them. To save the life of the baby Jesus from the hands of the murderous Herod, they bypass the scheming king and return home by a different route. They've been changed by their encounter with Jesus.

How have you been changed by Jesus? Might there be another road to which God is calling you?

Another road might require new imagination, investment, and resources. Another road might require new ways of sharing the depth of God's love for all creation. You might wonder whether you have what it takes.

God has what it takes, and God will provide abundantly all that is needed for God's dream of justice and peace to prevail. The baby born in Bethlehem is "the Alpha and the Omega, the first and the last, the beginning and the end" (Revelation 22:13). No matter where you are on this journey of faith, Jesus is with you.

Go in peace!

Prayer

We rest in you, faithful God. We expect you to lead us. We trust you to guide us to live at peace with you, with ourselves, and with one another. Thank you for loving this world so well. Amen.

Household Blessings and Prayers

Advent

In the days of Advent, Christians prepare to celebrate the presence of God's Word among us in our own day. During these four weeks, we pray that the reign of God, which Jesus preached and lived, would come among us. We pray that God's justice would flourish in our land, that the people of the earth would live in peace, that the weak and the sick and the hungry would be strengthened, healed, and fed with God's merciful presence.

During the last days of Advent, Christians welcome Christ with names inspired by the prophets: wisdom, liberator of slaves, mighty power, radiant dawn and sun of justice, the keystone of the arch of humanity, and Emmanuel—God with us.

The Advent wreath

One of the best-known customs for the season is the Advent wreath. The wreath and winter candle-lighting in the midst of growing darkness strengthen some of the Advent images found in the Bible. The unbroken circle of greens is clearly an image of everlasting life, a victory wreath, the crown of Christ, or the wheel of time itself. Christians use the wreath as a sign that Christ reaches into our time to lead us to the light of everlasting life. The four candles mark the progress of the four weeks of Advent and the growth of light. Sometimes the wreath is embellished with natural dried flowers or fruit. Its evergreen branches lead the household and the congregation to the evergreen Christmas tree. In many homes, the family gathers for prayer around the wreath.

An evening service of light for Advent

This brief order may be used on any evening during the season of Advent. If the household has an Advent wreath (one candle for each of the four weeks of Advent), it may be lighted during this service. Alternatively, one simple candle (perhaps a votive candle) may be lighted instead.

Lighting the Advent wreath
May this candle/these candles be a sign of the coming light of Christ.
One or more candles may be lighted.

Week 1: Lighting the first candle

Blessed are you, God of Jacob, for you promise to transform weapons of war into implements of planting and harvest and to teach us your way of peace; you promise that our night of sin is far gone and that your day of salvation is dawning.

As we light the first Advent candle, wake us from our sleep, wrap us in your light, empower us to live honorably, and guide us along your path of peace.

O house of Jacob, come,
let us walk in the light of the Lord. Amen.

Week 2: Lighting the first two candles

Blessed are you, God of hope, for you promise to bring forth a shoot from the stump of Jesse who will bring justice to the poor, who will deliver the needy and crush the oppressor, who will stand as a signal of hope for all people.

As we light these candles, turn our wills to bear the fruit of repentance, transform our hearts to live in justice and harmony with one another, and fix our eyes on the shoot from Jesse, Jesus Christ, the hope of all nations.

O people of hope, come,
let us rejoice in the faithfulness of the Lord. Amen.

Week 3: Lighting three candles
Blessed are you, God of might and majesty, for you promise to
make the desert rejoice and blossom, to watch over the strangers, and to set the prisoners free.

As we light these candles, satisfy our hunger with your good
gifts, open our eyes to the great things you have done for us,
and fill us with patience until the coming of the Lord Jesus.

O ransomed people of the Lord, come,
let us travel on God's holy way
and enter into Zion with singing. Amen.

Week 4: Lighting all four candles
Blessed are you, God of hosts, for you promised to send a Son,
Emmanuel, who brought your presence among us; and you
promise through your Son Jesus to save us from our sin.

As we light these candles, turn again to us in mercy;
strengthen our faith in the word spoken by your prophets;
restore us and give us life that we may be saved.

O house of David, come,
let us rejoice, for the Son of God, Emmanuel,
comes to be with us. Amen.

Reading
Read the scripture passage printed in the devotion for the day.

Hymn

One of the following hymns may be sung. The hymn might be accompanied by small finger cymbals.

"Light one candle to watch for Messiah," ELW 240
"People, look east," ELW 248
"Savior of the nations, come," ELW 263

During the final seven days of the Advent season (beginning December 17), the hymn "O come, O come, Emmanuel" (ELW 257) is particularly appropriate. The first stanza of the hymn could be sung each day during the final days before Christmas in addition to the stanza that is specifically appointed for the day. See pages 95–96 if you would like to use the hymn stanzas in the same order that the O Antiphons appear in this book.

First stanza
O come, O come, Emmanuel,
and ransom captive Israel,
that mourns in lonely exile here
until the Son of God appear.
Refrain Rejoice! Rejoice! Emmanuel shall come to you, O Israel.

December 17
O come, O Wisdom from on high,
embracing all things far and nigh:
in strength and beauty come and stay;
teach us your will and guide our way. *Refrain*

December 18

O come, O come, O Lord of might,
as to your tribes on Sinai's height
in ancient times you gave the law
in cloud, and majesty, and awe. *Refrain*

December 19

O come, O Branch of Jesse, free
your own from Satan's tyranny;
from depths of hell your people save,
and give them vict'ry o'er the grave. *Refrain*

December 20

O come, O Key of David, come,
and open wide our heav'nly home;
make safe the way that leads on high,
and close the path to misery. *Refrain*

December 21

O come, O Dayspring, come and cheer;
O Sun of justice, now draw near.
Disperse the gloomy clouds of night,
and death's dark shadow put to flight. *Refrain*

December 22

O come, O King of nations, come,
O Cornerstone that binds in one:
refresh the hearts that long for you;
restore the broken, make us new. *Refrain*

December 23

O come, O come, Emmanuel,
and ransom captive Israel,
that mourns in lonely exile here
until the Son of God appear. *Refrain*

Text: *Psalteriolum Cantionum Catholicarum*

Table prayer for Advent

Blessed are you, O Lord our God,
the one who is, who was, and who is to come.
At this table you fill us with good things.
May these gifts strengthen us
to share with the hungry and all those in need,
as we wait and watch for your coming among us
in Jesus Christ our Lord. Amen.

Christmas

Over the centuries, various customs have developed that focus the household on welcoming the light of Christ: the daily or weekly lighting of the Advent wreath, the blessing of the lighted Christmas tree, the candlelit procession of Las Posadas, the flickering lights of the luminaria, the Christ candle at Christmas.

The Christian household not only welcomes the light of Christ at Christmas but also celebrates the presence of that light throughout the Twelve Days, from Christmas until the Epiphany, January 6. In the Christmas season, Christians welcome the light of Christ that is already with us through faith. In word and gesture, prayer and song, in the many customs of diverse cultures, Christians celebrate this life-giving Word and ask that it dwell more deeply in the rhythm of daily life.

Lighting the Christmas tree

Use this prayer when you first illumine the tree or when you gather at the tree.

Holy God,
we praise you as we light this tree.
It gives light to this place
as you shine light into darkness through Jesus,
the light of the world.
God of all,

we thank you for your love,
the love that has come to us in Jesus.
Be with us now as we remember that gift of love,
and help us to share that love with a yearning world.
Creator God,
you made the stars in the heavens.
Thank you for the light that shines on us in Jesus,
the bright morning star.
Amen.

Blessing of the nativity scene

*This blessing may be used when figures are added to the nativity
scene and throughout the days of Christmas.*

Bless us, O God, as we remember a humble birth. With each
angel and shepherd we place here before you, show us the
wonder found in a stable. In song and prayer, silence and awe,
we adore your gift of love, Christ Jesus our Savior. Amen.

Table prayer for the twelve days of Christmas (December 25–January 5)

With joy and gladness we feast upon your love, O God.
You have come among us in Jesus, your Son,
and your presence now graces this table.
May Christ dwell in us
that we might bear his love to all the world,
for he is Lord forever and ever. Amen.

Epiphany

On the Epiphany of Our Lord (January 6), the household joins the church throughout the world in celebrating the manifestation, the "epiphany," of Christ to the world. The festival of Christmas is thus set within the context of outreach to the larger community; it possesses an outward movement. The festival of the Epiphany asks the Christian household: How might our faith in Christ the Light be shared with friends and family, with our neighbors, with the poor and needy in our land, with those who live in other nations?

Blessing for a home

Matthew writes that when the magi saw the shining star stop overhead, they were filled with joy. "On entering the house, they saw the child with Mary his mother" (Matthew 2:11). In the home, Christ is met in family and friends, in visitors and strangers. In the home, faith is shared, nurtured, and put into action. In the home, Christ is welcome.

Twelfth Night (January 5), Epiphany of Our Lord (January 6), or another day during the time after Epiphany offers an occasion for gathering with friends and family members for a blessing of the home. Someone may lead the greeting and blessing, while another person may read the scripture passage. Following an Eastern European tradition, a visual blessing may be inscribed with white chalk above the main door; for example, 20 + CMB + 24. The numbers change with each new year. The three letters stand for either the ancient Latin blessing Christe mansionem benedicat, *which means "Christ, bless this house," or the legendary names of the magi (Caspar, Melchior, and Balthasar).*

Greeting
Peace to this house and to all who enter here.
By wisdom a house is built,
and through understanding it is established;
through knowledge its rooms are filled
with rare and beautiful treasures. (*Proverbs 24:3-4*)

Reading
As we prepare to ask God's blessing on this household,
let us listen to the words of scripture.
In the beginning was the Word,
and the Word was with God, and the Word was God.
He was in the beginning with God.
All things came into being through him,
and without him not one thing came into being.
What has come into being in him was life,
and the life was the light of all people.
The Word became flesh and lived among us, and we have seen his glory,
the glory as of a father's only son, full of grace and truth.
From his fullness we have all received grace upon grace.
(*John 1:1-4, 14, 16*)

Inscription

This inscription may be made with chalk above the entrance:

20 + C M B + 24

Write the appropriate character (left) while speaking the text (right).

The magi of old, known as

C   Caspar,

M   Melchior, and

B   Balthasar,

followed the star of God's Son who came to dwell among us

20   two thousand

24   and twenty-four years ago.

+   Christ, bless this house,

+   and remain with us throughout the new year.

Prayer of Blessing

O God,

you revealed your Son to all people by the shining light of a star.

We pray that you bless this home and all who live here
with your gracious presence.

May your love be our inspiration, your wisdom our guide,
your truth our light, and your peace our benediction;
through Christ our Lord. Amen.

Then everyone may walk from room to room, blessing the house with incense or by sprinkling with water, perhaps using a branch from the Christmas tree.

Table prayer for Epiphany

Generous God,
you have made yourself known in Jesus, the light of the world.
As this food and drink give us refreshment,
so strengthen us by your spirit,
that as your baptized sons and daughters
we may share your light with all the world.
Grant this through Christ our Lord.
Amen.

Notes

Welcome: *Psalteriolum Cantionum Catholicarum*, Köln, 1710; tr. composite, sts. 2, 6, 7 © 1997 Augsburg Fortress, "O come, O come, Emmanuel," ELW 257, st. 1. **December 3:** "O Antiphons," traditional, para. Elise Feyerherm, in *Music Sourcebook for All Saints through Transfiguration* (Minneapolis: Augsburg Fortress, 2013), S539. Hymn text: "O come, O come, Emmanuel," ELW 257, st. 2. **December 4:** Sri Chinmoy, *Life-Tree Leaves* (Jamaica, NY: Agni, 1974), www.srichinmoylibrary.com/ltl. **December 7:** Text: William C. Dix, 1837–1898, "What child is this," ELW 296, st. 2. **December 8:** "O Antiphons," *Music Sourcebook.* "O come, O come, Emmanuel," ELW 257, st. 3. **December 9:** Brené Brown, *The Gifts of Imperfection* (Center City, MN: Hazelden, 2020), 70. **December 10:** Michaeleen Doucleff, *Hunt, Gather, Parent* (New York: Avid Reader, 2021), 208. **December 11:** bell hooks, *All About Love* (New York: HarperCollins, 2001), 34. **December 12:** Chinook Prayer, Pacific Northwest Coast, www.xavier.edu/jesuitresource/online-resources/prayer-index/native-american. **December 13:** "O Antiphons," *Music Sourcebook.* "O come, O come, Emmanuel," ELW 257, st. 4. **December 14:** Text: Jean Janzen, b. 1933, based on Hildegard of Bingen, 1098–1179, © Jean Janzen, admin. Augsburg Fortress, "O Holy Spirit, root of life," ELW 399, st. 1. **December 15:** "Do Not Fear," in Walter Brueggemann, *Awed to Heaven, Rooted in Earth* (Minneapolis: Fortress, 2003), 93. **December 16:** Gustavo Gutierrez, *A Theology of*

Liberation (Maryknoll, NY: Orbis, 1973), 205. **December 17:** Peter Wohlleben, trans. Jane Billinghurst, *The Hidden Life of Trees* (Vancouver/Berkeley: Greystone, 2016), 18. **December 18:** "O Antiphons," *Music Sourcebook.* "O come, O come, Emmanuel," ELW 257, st. 5. Confession and Forgiveness, *ELW*, 95, 117. **December 20:** Isaac of Syria, also known as Isaac of Nineveh, https://blogs.ancientfaith.com/glory2god forallthings/2006/11/01/words-from-st-isaac-of-syria/. **December 21:** Holy Baptism, *ELW*, 231. **December 22:** Text: Medieval Latin carol; tr. John Mason Neale, 1818–1866, "Good Christian friends, rejoice," ELW 288, st. 2. **December 23:** "O Antiphons," *Music Sourcebook.* "O come, O come, Emmanuel," ELW 257, st. 1. **December 24:** Text: Martin Luther, 1483–1546; tr. *Lutheran Book of Worship*, admin. Augsburg Fortress, "From heaven above," ELW 268, st. 4. **December 25:** Text: Liturgy of St. James; tr. Gerard Moultrie, 1829–1885, alt., "Let all mortal flesh keep silence," ELW 490, st. 3. **December 26:** Text: Josua Stegmann, 1588–1632; tr. August Crull, 1846–1923; "Abide, O dearest Jesus," ELW 539, st. 4. **December 27:** Text: Anonymous, Central America; tr. Gerhard M. Cartford, b. 1923–2016, English text © 1998 Augsburg Fortress; "The Lord now sends us forth," ELW 538. **December 28:** "O Antiphons," *Music Sourcebook.* "O come, O come, Emmanuel," ELW 257, st. 6. **December 29:** Isaac S. Villegas, "A Shower in the Desert," *The Christian Century*, December 14, 2022, www.christiancentury.org/article/voices /shower-desert). **December 30:** Ocean Vuong, "The

Weight of Our Living," *The Rumpus*, 20 December 2022, https://therumpus.net/2022/12/20/the-weight-of-our-living-on-hope-fire-escapes-and-visible-desperation/). **December 31:** Wendell Berry, in Amanda Petrusich, "Going Home with Wendell Berry," *The New Yorker*, July 14, 2019, www.newyorker.com/culture/the-new-yorker-interview/going-home-with-wendell-berry. **January 1:** Jeff Chu, "Arranging the Flowers," *Notes of a Make-Believe Farmer* blog, October 13, 2022, https://jeffchu.substack.com/p/arranging-the-flowers). **January 2:** "O Antiphons," *Music Sourcebook.* "O come, O come, Emmanuel," ELW 257, st. 7. **January 3:** Martin Luther, trans. Timothy J. Wengert, *Luther's Small Catechism* (Minneapolis: Augsburg Fortress, 2016). **January 4:** Jacqui Lewis, *Fierce Love* (New York: Harmony, 2021), 176. **January 5:** Morgan Harper Nichols, *Peace Is a Practice* (Grand Rapids, MI: Zondervan, 2022), 216. **January 6:** Barbara Bash, *True Nature* (Boston: Shambhala, 2004), 82. **Pages 93-94:** "O come, O come, Emmanuel," ELW 257.

Singing "O come, O come, Emmanuel" during your devotional time

The first stanza of the hymn "O come, O come, Emmanuel" can be sung in addition to the stanza that aligns with the O Antiphon assigned to each day.

First stanza

O come, O come, Emmanuel,
and ransom captive Israel,
that mourns in lonely exile here
until the Son of God appear.
Refrain Rejoice! Rejoice! Emmanuel shall come to you, O Israel.

December 3–7

O come, O Wisdom from on high,
embracing all things far and nigh:
in strength and beauty come and stay;
teach us your will and guide our way. *Refrain*

December 8–12

O come, O come, O Lord of might,
as to your tribes on Sinai's height
in ancient times you gave the law
in cloud, and majesty, and awe. *Refrain*

December 13–17

O come, O Branch of Jesse, free
your own from Satan's tyranny;
from depths of hell your people save,
and give them vict'ry o'er the grave. *Refrain*

December 18–22

O come, O Key of David, come,
and open wide our heav'nly home;
make safe the way that leads on high,
and close the path to misery. *Refrain*

December 23–27

O come, O come, Emmanuel,
and ransom captive Israel,
that mourns in lonely exile here
until the Son of God appear. *Refrain*

December 28–January 1

O come, O Dayspring, come and cheer;
O Sun of justice, now draw near.
Disperse the gloomy clouds of night,
and death's dark shadow put to flight. *Refrain*

January 2–6

O come, O King of nations, come,
O Cornerstone that binds in one:
refresh the hearts that long for you;
restore the broken, make us new. *Refrain*